Manifest Destiny of American Exceptionalism:

The policies which maintain our chart topping performance in every measurable category.

Sarcaustic913 Publishing

Table of Contents

Preface

This book is intended to shed light on the often cloak and dagger nature of American Politics. By nearly every metric the United States is at the top of the world; inside these pages are the policies that have made this country Exceptional, and will allow it to remain so. Any argument to the contrary is merely insidious drivel.

For nearly two hundred fifty years the United States of America has provided the universal definition of Exceptional. In order to assist the growing number of countries which find themselves in the nearly irreversible slide to third world status, it is time that the manner in which we have maintained our superiority be disclosed.

At the close of our 57th election cycle the American people are finally able to proclaim that we have our politics down to a science. American politics are meticulously conducted with attention given to all opinions, it is for this reason we are certain our Exceptionalism will never falter. Our tradition of comprehensive deliberation and debate of the issues allows us the opportunity to successfully coalesce around the candidate with the most enduring and optimistic vision for the future of our Nation. It is with humble pride and resolution of purpose that we formally address these important issues every four years. We recognize that it is this continual consideration of issues that allows us to have steadfast policies in the face of growing international turmoil.

In this book I have sought to distill to their very essence the policies by which my fellow Americans and I have unwaveringly chosen to run our country. Stripping away the political wordsmanship reveals the depth of thought necessary to achieve the level of success that has made the United States of America the greatest nation in the world.

My Grandparents Weren't Apes!
I'm NOT paying for YOUR education.
School Choice
Put GOD back in school!
Stop REVERSE DISCRIMINATION

Chapter 1

~ ~ ~

Education

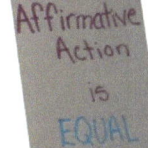

I support the
2nd Ammendment,
where's my
NUKE?

First Class
CITIZENSHIP
for ALL
legalize gay marriage

Don't hold the
ALIEN-ship
of my parents
against my
CITIZENSHIP

Planned
Parenthood
SAVES lives

Legalize

Chapter 2

~ ~ ~

Justice

What God Made Man Can Not Destroy

NATURAL GAS for Energy Independance

Hummer 4 Life

Drill BABY DRILL

CLEAN COAL

Chapter 3

~ ~ ~

Environment

Save
the
Economy
Increase
Wages

When you can slap
it to Ol' Sparky...
THEN It's
a PERSON

Business
without
Regulation
Kills

Fair
Trade

Coffee

Organized
Labor
Benefits
EveryOne

Chapter 4

~ ~ ~

Business

Better dead than **RED**

Privitize Social Security + Medicare

Poverty is a Necessary Incentive for Work..

Welfare  Independance

I'm not paying for you to be lazy!

Chapter 5

~ ~ ~

Social Services

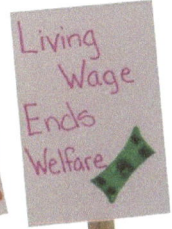
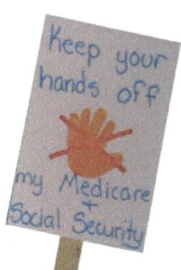

Tax Speculation

Paying taxes is your Membership to this Country Club

Pay down the debt Increase Taxes

TAX the 1%

Do we really need more Hotel Heiresses?

Chapter 6

~ ~ ~

Taxation

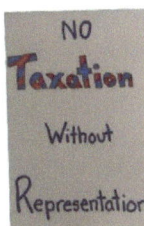

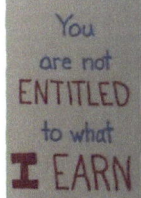

There is
a reason
it's called
the
Patriot Act

Support
Troops

There is no
such thing
as an
OVERSIZED
Military.

Waterboarding
is like
swimming
in the
kiddie pool
of Safety.

Striking 1ˢᵗ
saves
American
lives

Chapter 7

~ ~ ~

National Defense

Ratify **KYOTO** Protocol

Reauthorize Test Ban Treaty

WHO saves lives

Increase Foreign Aid
It's a small price to pay for friends.

Muslims **ARE** welcome here
Say **NO** to racist fear

Chapter 8

~ ~ ~

International Affairs

Conclusion

See? I told you so.

Let the CELEBRATION begin!

Drop the Confetti!

Cue the Balloons!

Start the Fireworks!

Strike up the Band!

All together now,

SING!

America
the
Beautiful

My Country 'tis of Thee

This

Land

is

Your

Land

Battle Hymn of The Republic

When Johnny Comes Marching Home Again

Star

Spangled

Banner

You're
A Grand
Old
Flag

Washing
-ton
Post
March

God

Bless

The

U.S.A.

Stars
and
Stripes
Forever

I would like to send a special word of thanks to my fellow Americans for making this book possible.
And most especially to:

Your Name Here

And

May God

Continue to Bless the

United States of America!